FISHING SKILLS

Pike Fishing

Tony Whieldon

Introduction by Jim Gibbinson

WARD LOCK LIMITED · LONDON

© Ward Lock Limited 1987

First published in Great Britain in 1987
by Ward Lock Limited, 8 Clifford Street
London W1X 1RB, an Egmont Company.

Printed and bound in Italy by New Interlitho, Milan

British Library Cataloguing in Publication Data

Whieldon, Tony
  Pike fishing. ——— (Fishing skills)
  1. Pike fishing
  I. Title   II. Series
  799.1'753   SH691.P6

ISBN 0-7063-6551-8

Contents

Acknowledgments
My thanks to Barry Jackiw of Exeter
Angling Centre for help with plug
reference, and also to Jim
Gibbinson for reference on various
other subjects.

Introduction

Is there any fish in freshwater that evokes such passions as the pike? For every pike lover who regards them as the most exciting quarry of all, there is a pike hater who sees them as a threat to other fish stocks. Every year at angling club annual meetings there are heated arguments between those who want pike preserved and those who want them killed. Everyone has strong views; there are few indifferent bystanders.

So what is the truth? As a self-confessed pike addict I have to concede that my views are likely to be biased, but I cannot understand why a fish that has lived in harmony with other species for something like 60 million years should suddenly become a threat! Experience suggests that problems only occur when anglers upset nature's balance by embarking on a pike removal policy; if sizeable pike are removed from a water there will be less cannibalistic predation, which in turn results in a higher than usual survival rate of the annual crop of pike-fry. If, however, all sizeable pike are returned alive to the water they successfully keep their own fry in check. This is not merely personal opinion but is supported by the findings of the Freshwater Biological Association in Windermere and the Inland Fisheries Trust in Ireland.

Anti-pike prejudice is widespread, so preservation must be the first priority of every pike enthusiast. A positive step towards this end is to attend club AGMs to try to prevent the introduction of pike removal policies.

I am not one of those who argue that pike are actually good for a fishery – I know plenty of good waters that hold no pike at all – but I do not believe that they are bad for a water either. The reason I want to see them safeguarded is because they are beautiful fish and provide for most anglers their best chance of catching something of rod-bending proportions. Look at it this way: a 3 kg pike is a very modest fish – even the poorest of waters will produce pike of such a size – but what are the chances of an angler catching other species of that weight? Most anglers have never even seen tench, chub, bream or barbel of 3 kg, let alone caught one! Only carp compare with pike for size, but they are very much more difficult to catch and geographically are rather limited in their distribution. Pike, on the other hand, are widespread – no matter where you live you are bound to have pike fishing fairly near at hand. They are a very adaptable fish too – they can be found in lakes, gravel pits, lochs (loughs in Ireland), reservoirs, ponds, canals, rivers and streams – and no matter where they are found, they are capable of growing very large. I have caught pike in excess of 25 lb (11.3 kg) from waters comparable in size to the average village duck-pond – in fact I know of a 30-pounder (13.6 kg) that actually came from a village duck-pond! I am not suggesting that village ponds are the most likely locations for big pike, but merely making the point that quite modest waters can hold surprisingly large fish.

Once you start reading pike fishing literature you will find it rich in folklore, especially on the subject of how large they grow. I recall talking to one avid pike fan who was convinced that their maximum size was over 100 lb (45.3 kg)! Even the legendary Loch Kenmure 72-pounder (32.6 kg) reported in *The Sporting Magazine* in 1798 palls into insignificance by comparison! I think it more probable that the 'ceiling' is in the region of 50 lb (22.6 kg), because the largest well-authenticated specimens my reading has revealed have been one of 50½ lb (22.9 kg) and another of 48 lb (21.7 kg). These were netted from Lough Sheelin by the Inland Fisheries Trust, in the course of their ill-advised Trout Improvement Scheme. A close contender in recent years was a fish that was caught several times from the River Thurne. This currently heads the National Coarse Fish Record List at 42 lb 2 oz (19.1 kg), this weight having been recorded when it was caught by Derek Amies in 1985. There was also an impressive recent claim of 44 lb (19.9 kg) for an Ardleigh Reservoir fish, taken by Michael Linton in January 1987. (At the time of writing the result of this record claim is not known).

Few of us aspire to the dizzy heights of 40-pounders (18.1 kg) and many experienced pike anglers have yet to see a fish of even half that weight. However, with luck and persistence the keen pike angler can reasonably hope to top 20 lb (9 kg) once or twice in his career, but 30-pounders (13.6 kg) will probably remain the fish of dreams. I have caught lots of 20-pounders and have come to within ounces of 30 lb, but I have yet to see the needle of my balance go past that magic mark. One close friend of mine, however, has five such fish to his credit, which proves that dreams *can* come true!

Whatever your aspirations and whatever your level of experience, you will find a lot of valuable advice and information in the pages of this book. Tony Whieldon has distilled the best of traditional and modern knowledge – including some of the very latest developments such as long range drift-fishing with vaned floats – and compiled a comprehensive guide to pike fishing in all types of water. You will not, however, find any guidance on how to use livebaits. Tony Whieldon has taken a stance on this issue and decided that it would be wrong to include information on a method to which he has strong personal objections. Some may regard this as an omission while others, myself included, applaud his decision. Livebaiting is cruel, and no amount of rationalizing on the part of those who want the practice to continue will alter that fact. Nor is it necessary to use livebaits in order to be a successful pike angler – I have not used livebaits for about ten years but I catch plenty of pike, including my share of big ones. It would, of course, be naive to suggest that there are never days when livebaiting might be the most effective method – such days are bound to occur, but they occur a lot less frequently than the supporters of livebaiting would have you believe. In any event, cruelty is indefensible, so arguments as to the importance of the method in the angler's repertoire are therefore irrelevant.

If you use lures and deadbaits in the ways Tony Whieldon describes you will catch plenty of pike – that I promise you. One day you will hopefully experience the thrill of seeing a metre or more of yellow rolling in the waves as you draw over your landing-net a fish bigger and more powerful than anything you've caught previously. Unhook it, take a couple of souvenir photos and return it carefully to the water. Pike are magnificent fish – please treat them with care and accord respect to the waters from which you catch them. Pike have been around for a long, long time – let us ensure that they are around for a long time to come.

Jim Gibbinson
Cuxton, Kent.

February 1987

Popular pike spots

NORFOLK
BROADS

LOCH
LOMOND

FENLAND
DRAINS

LOCH
CONN

RIVER
TRENT

SLAPTON
LEY

CANALS

RIVER
WYE

ESTATE
PONDS

FLOODED
GRAVEL
PITS

RESERVOIRS

Pike

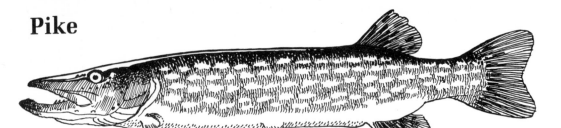

The pike (*Esox lucius*) is widespread throughout the northern latitudes in lowland rivers and lakes. Adult pike feed mainly on fish, although occasionally frogs, water voles and young water birds are also eaten.

The body markings of a pike provide ideal camouflage among weeds and sub-surface plant stems, where it lies in ambush. Body colouring varies, but is generally made up of browns, olives and greens, with yellow or gold flecks or bars along the flanks, and a white or cream belly. The rear fins are flecked and sometimes tinted crimson.

The eyes of the pike are set high in the head, providing good upward vision. Shallow grooves running from the eye to the snout permit clear forward vision, necessary to all predators.

The pike's dorsal and anal fin are set well to the rear of the body, immediately in front of the tail fin. This combination of fin-power provides enough acceleration to grasp any small fish which may come within striking distance.

Pike can grow very large, even in small waters, provided that fodder fish are plentiful. Monsters of over 40lb (18 kg) have been caught, but a 20lb (9 kg) pike is worthy of merit.

Lure fishing

Artificial bait fishing with plugs, spoons and spinners is the most exciting and sporting method of catching pike. Natural baits, as a rule, will account for larger pike, but lures definitely produce greater numbers of fish.

Rods

The rod on the left is a 7ft (2·15m) baitcasting rod for use with plugs. On the right is a 9ft (2·75m) 1½ lb (0·70 kg) test curve spinning rod for fishing spoons, spinners and larger plugs. Rod rings should be large in diameter and lined with one of the new, low-friction ceramic materials.

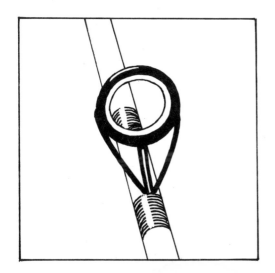

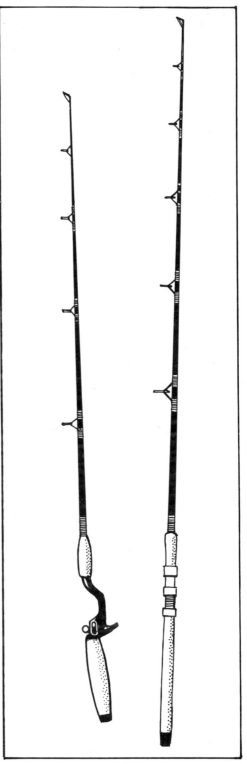

Reels for lure fishing

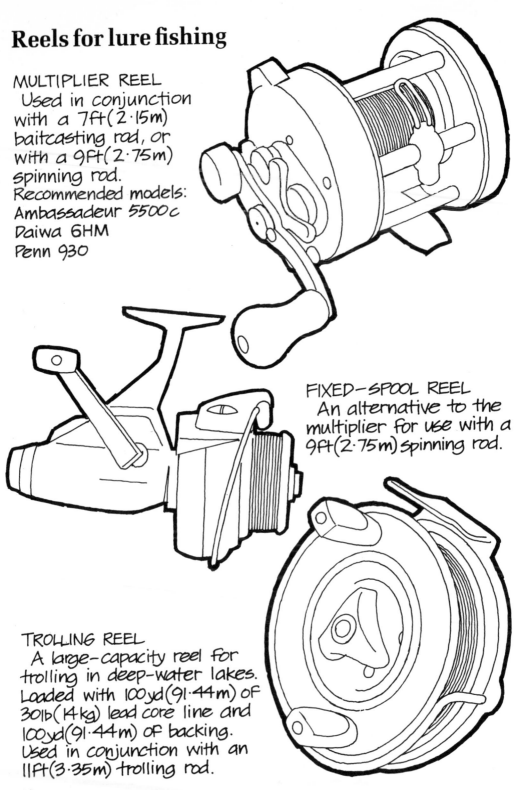

MULTIPLIER REEL
  Used in conjunction
with a 7ft(2·15m)
baitcasting rod, or
with a 9ft(2·75m)
spinning rod.
Recommended models:
Ambassadeur 5500c
Daiwa 6HM
Penn 930

FIXED-SPOOL REEL
  An alternative to the
multiplier for use with a
9ft(2·75m) spinning rod.

TROLLING REEL
  A large-capacity reel for
trolling in deep-water lakes.
Loaded with 100yd(91·44m) of
30lb(14kg) lead core line and
100yd(91·44m) of backing.
Used in conjunction with an
11ft(3·35m) trolling rod.

Terminal tackle for lures

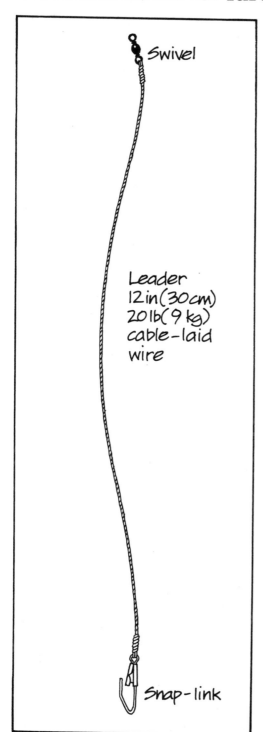

Swivel

Leader
12 in (30 cm)
20 lb (9 kg)
cable-laid
wire

Snap-link

Although wire leaders can be purchased ready-made, it is a simple matter to make your own, and cut down the cost into the bargain.

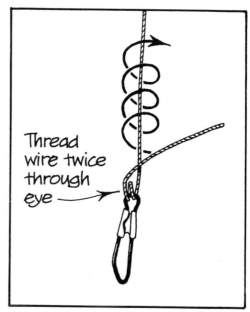

Thread
wire twice
through
eye

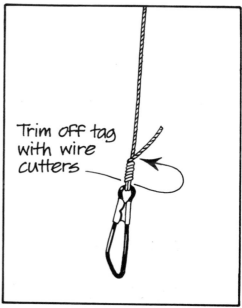

Trim off tag
with wire
cutters

Spoons

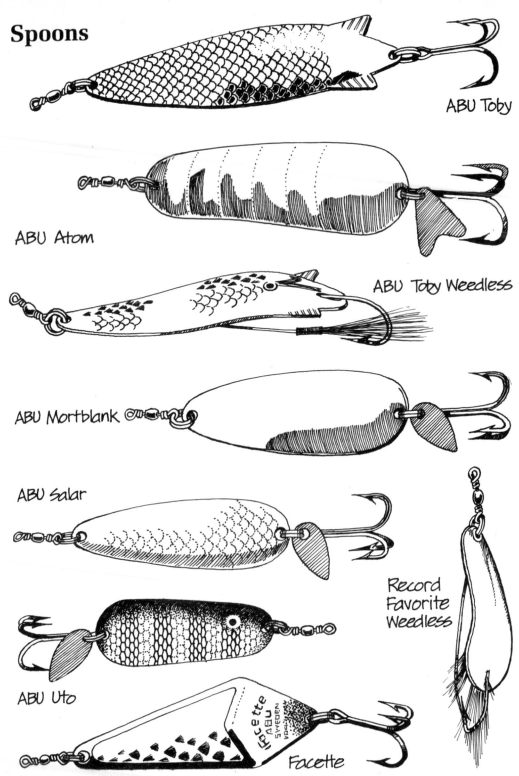

ABU Toby

ABU Atom

ABU Toby Weedless

ABU Mortblank

ABU Salar

ABU Uto

Record
Favorite
Weedless

Facette

Plugs

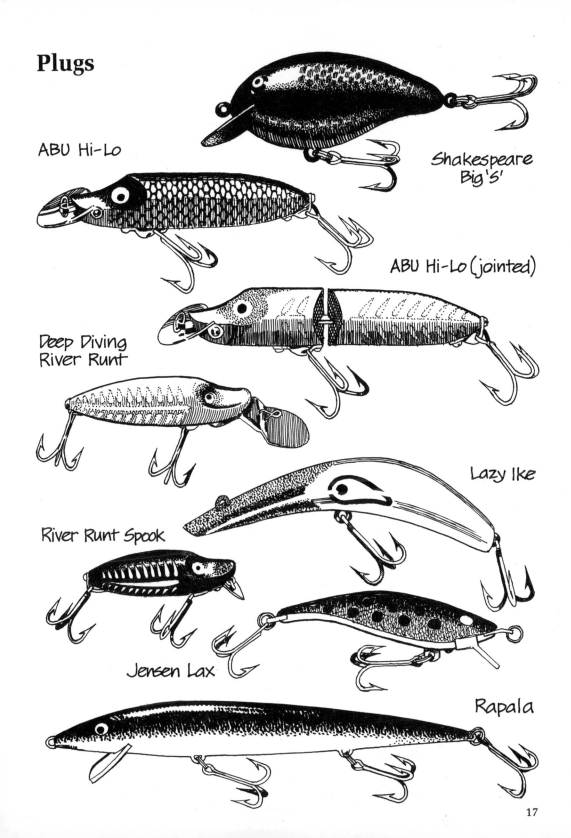

ABU Hi-Lo

Shakespeare Big 'S'

ABU Hi-Lo (jointed)

Deep Diving River Runt

Lazy Ike

River Runt Spook

Jensen Lax

Rapala

More about plugs

SURFACE PLUGS skitter and pop along the surface of the water when they are retrieved.

FLOATING PLUGS float on the surface when stationary, dive and wriggle when retrieved, then rise towards the surface again when the retrieve is slowed or stopped.

Some plugs have an adjustable vane.

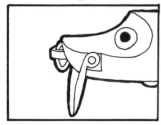 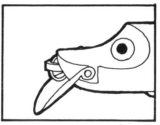 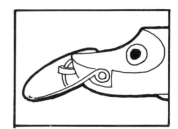

On or near surface   Shallow dive   Very steep dive

SINKING PLUGS sink slowly to the required depth and dive and wriggle when retrieved. These plugs are ideal for searching out the deeper-lying fish.

Spinners

ABU Reflex

Bucktail Toni

ABU Droppen

Shakespeare Kilko

Daiwa
Victor

Mepps Nº4

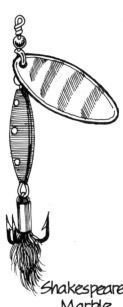

Shakespeare
Marble

Plugs

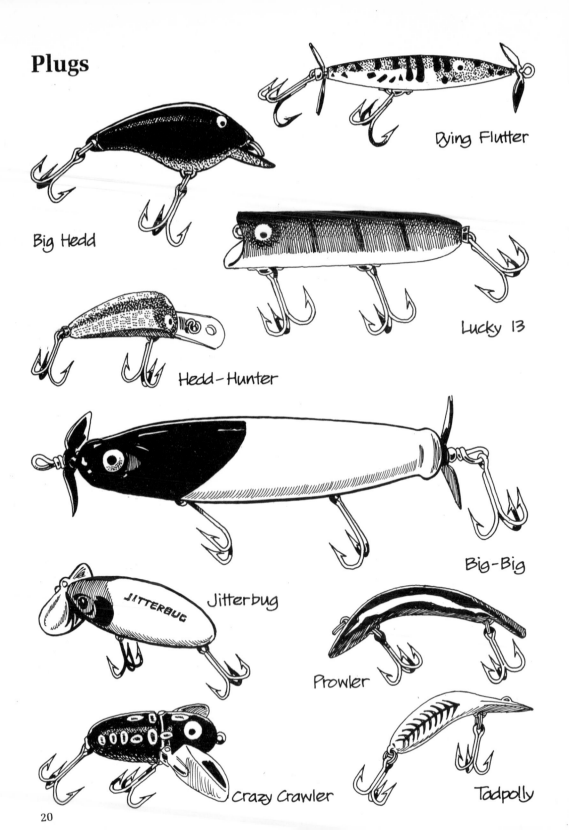

Dying Flutter

Big Hedd

Lucky 13

Hedd-Hunter

Jitterbug

Big-Big

Prowler

Crazy Crawler

Tadpolly

Spoons, spinners and plugs

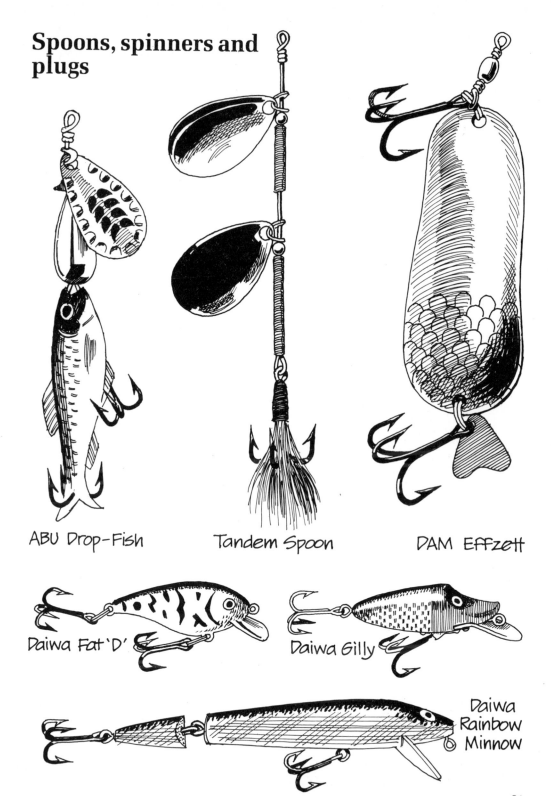

ABU Drop-Fish

Tandem Spoon

DAM Effzett

Daiwa Fat 'D'

Daiwa Gilly

Daiwa Rainbow Minnow

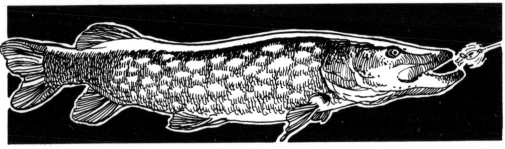

Lure fishing

The best time to commence any form of pike fishing is with the approach of autumn, and to cease at the end of February.

Lure Fishing is a mobile occupation, therefore the angler should travel light. One or two rods, a carp-size landing net, a rucksack containing a selection of lures, hook removal equipment, and a hot drink and food are the only important items needed.

Optional extras such as a spring balance or a camera can also be included.

A waterproof jacket and thermal underwear will ensure maximum comfort if the weather is cold, and thermal-lined waterproof boots will permit unhindered walking from spot-to-spot — waders can be worn but are rather cumbersome. Warm headwear will also be needed to retain the body heat.

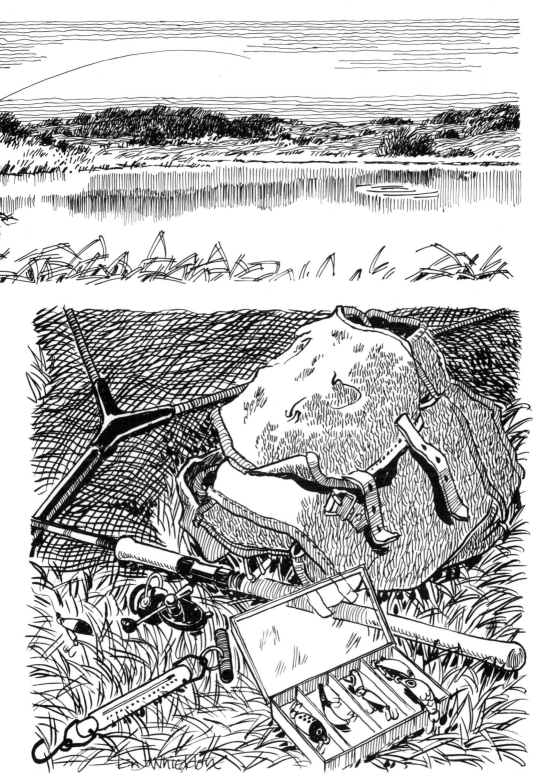

Lure fishing in lakes

Pike, like any other fish, are not distributed evenly over the lake or river. Recognition of potential pike-holding areas will save much futile casting. The diagram shows the types of places where the pike fisherman is likely to encounter his quarry when fishing a lake.

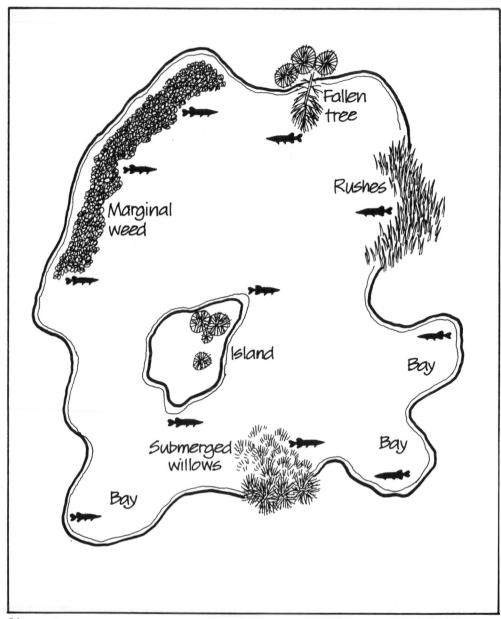

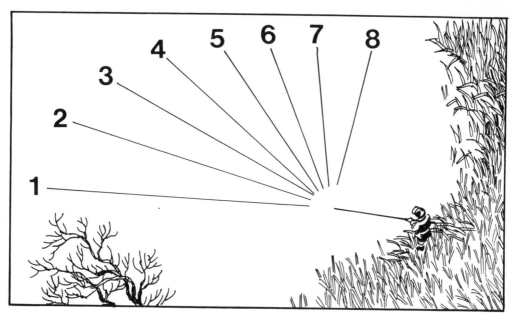

Likely-looking areas in lakes should be fished methodically, letting the lure cover as much water as possible.

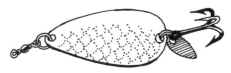

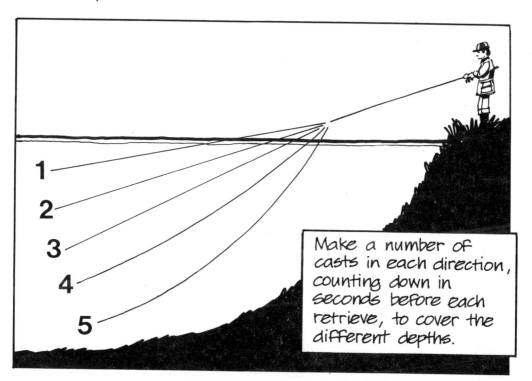

Make a number of casts in each direction, counting down in seconds before each retrieve, to cover the different depths.

If the weather is fine and sunny during September or October, pike may sometimes be seen basking close to the bank. A small lure, cast just to the rear of the fish will usually get an instant response.

Before the winter frosts have killed off the weed, some shallow bays may have a thick sub-surface growth which completely covers the bottom, leaving an area of clear water above it. These areas may look fishless, but it is always worth casting a surface, or shallow-diving, plug into such areas, for pike often hide in the weed.

With the progress of winter and the lowering of surface water temperatures, pike will be inclined to move towards the deeper areas of the lake, where the water is warmer, and where smaller food fish will be concentrated.

Knowledge of the lake-bed contours is invaluable, and the angler who lives close at hand can take the time to plumb the depths during the warmer months. A plan can then be drawn to show the likely fish-holding spots.

This method of depth-finding is only practical on relatively small lakes; larger areas of water, ones that would be fished from a boat, would require an echo sounder.

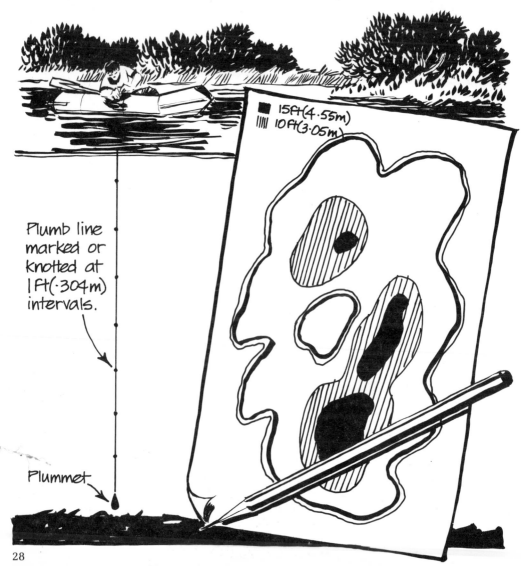

Plumb line marked or knotted at 1ft(·304m) intervals.

Plummet

15ft(4·55m)
10ft(3·05m)

Deep-water area

Fan out casts, to cover deep areas methodically and thoroughly.

When fishing these deeper areas of water from the shore, long-distance casting is often required. A 9ft (2·75 m) rod in conjunction with a fairly heavy spoon lure is the ideal combination. Work the spoon back slowly, and deeply.

Lure fishing in rivers

Rivers provide an exciting challenge to the lure angler, with their varying currents and underwater obstacles and snags.

An ability to 'read' the water and recognize the potential pike-holding areas is necessary to ensure consistent success.

Likely pike-holding spots

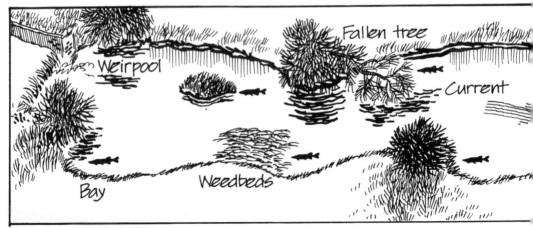

Weirpool · Fallen tree · Current · Bay · Weedbeds

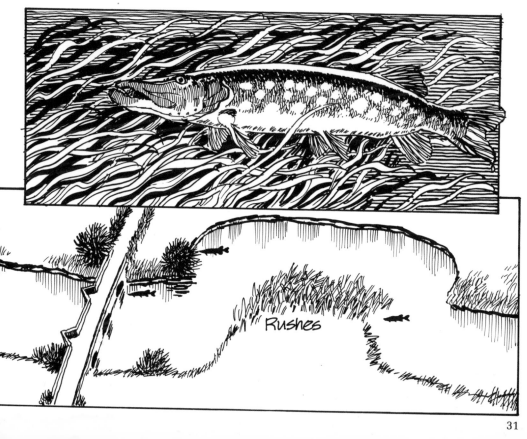

Rushes

Kinking line can be a problem when fishing with spoons and spinners, especially on rivers, where the current tends to aggravate the situation. A variety of devices can be used to help eliminate this problem. Probably the most efficient is a ball bearing swivel which has a detachable, rigid, transparent vane. This is connected to the terminal tackle in the position shown.

Anti-kink leads also help to eliminate line twist, and hold the lure deeper in the water. However, it is best to use only the smaller sizes when a lure is being cast, as too much weight up-trace may result in the trace doubling back and wrapping itself around the main line.

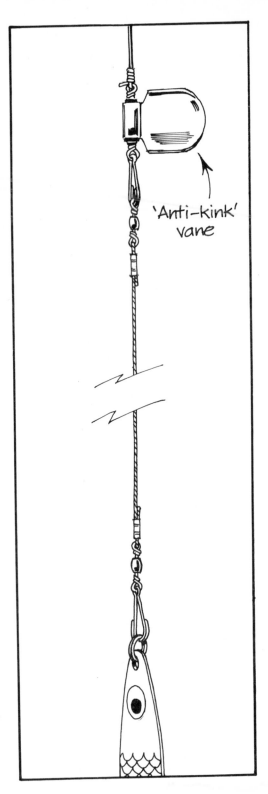

'Anti-kink' vane

 FOLD OVER LEADS

 WYE LEAD

 SPIRAL LEAD

 KEEL LEAD

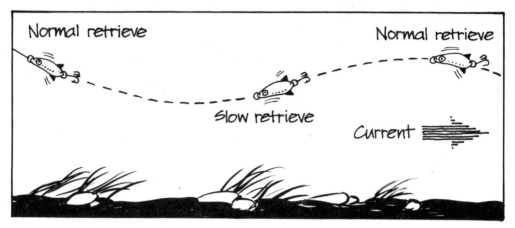

Normal retrieve

Normal retrieve

Slow retrieve

Current

Fishing a river with a lure is not simply a matter of casting and retrieving. The lure should be worked through the water by using different retrieve speeds in order to create the impression of a natural fish. At times, the lure should be allowed to tumble back, down current.

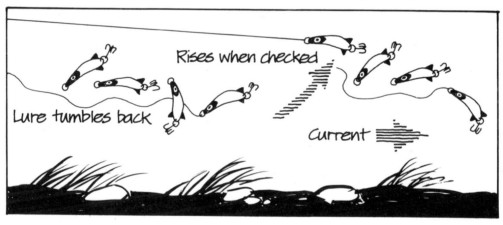

Rises when checked

Lure tumbles back

Current

The closer a lure can be presented to the lie of a river pike, the better.

When a likely-looking or well known hot-spot has been located, it should be fished very thoroughly. The lure should be presented at all depths, especially close to the bank, where the larger pike are often lying in ambush.

Eddies are always worth special attention, especially if the river is fining down after a heavy flood.

MAIN CURRENT

EDDY

X Pike most likely
to be here

Where there is a good depth of water beneath the fishing position the lure should be fished almost back to the rod tip. Pike will often follow the lure without taking. If a pike is seen doing this, the retrieve should be speeded up, where-upon the pike will usually make a grab for the lure and become firmly hooked.

Fishing a natural deadbait

Judging by the weekly reports in 'Angler's Mail' it would seem that the majority of pike captures come as a result of using dead fish as bait, as opposed to livebaits.

Deadbaits such as mackerel, sprats and herrings are easily obtainable from fishmongers or fish quays, and can be stored in a deep freeze until they are needed. Freshwater species such as roach, rudd and bleak can be caught on light tackle during the warmer months, killed humanely, and stored in the same way as sea fish.

Whether this general trend towards deadbaits is as a result of the availability of freezer units, or a conversion towards a more sensitive and moralistic consideration for the bait-fish I cannot say; but I would hope that it is the latter.

DEADBAIT SPECIES

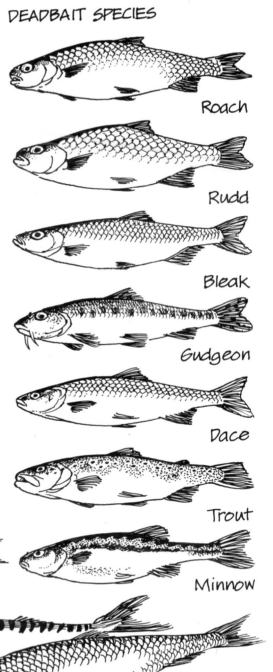

Roach

Rudd

Bleak

Gudgeon

Dace

Trout

Sprat

Minnow

Mackerel

Herring

36

Deadbait trace

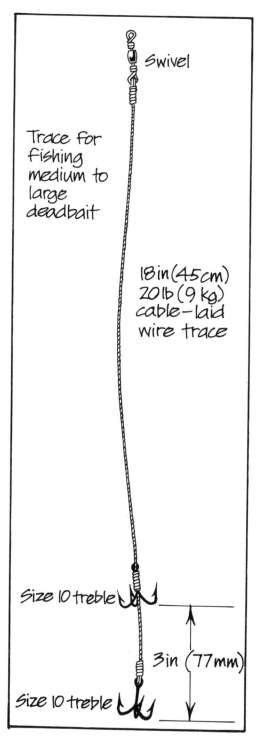

Swivel

Trace for
fishing
medium to
large
deadbait

18in (45cm)
20lb (9 kg)
cable-laid
wire trace

Size 10 treble

3in (77mm)

Size 10 treble

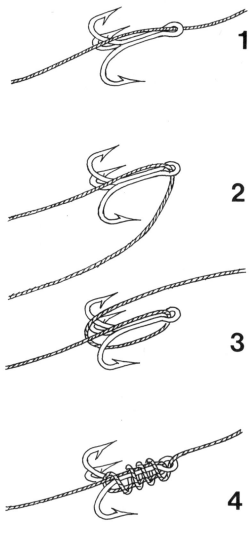

1

2

3

4

The sequence above shows
the Jim Gibbinson method
for tying on the up-trace
treble, which should always be
tied first. The lower hook
and swivel can then be tied
on by using the method
shown in the lure trace page.
Traces with one treble can
also be made for fishing
small baits.

Mounting deadbaits

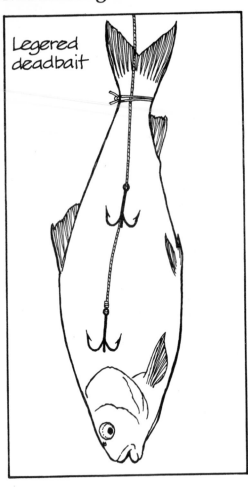

Legered
deadbait

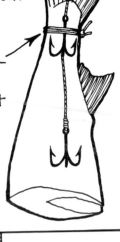

Half fish
legered deadbait

Tie with mono-
Filament line,
to prevent bait
Flying off
during cast.

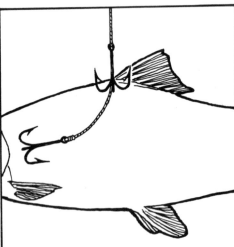

Float-paternoster set-up

Small deadbait

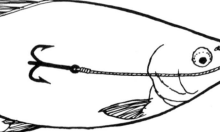

Wobble bait

The deadbait rod

The ideal deadbait rod needs a good backbone to contend with the pressure it has to sustain. A length of 11ft (3.35m) with a test curve of 2½lb (1.15kg) to 3lb (1.35kg) will be adequate.

Line with a breaking strain of 12lb (5.50kg) is sufficiently strong in normal conditions but something heavier may have to be used where snags or dense weed occur.

Fishing a legered deadbait

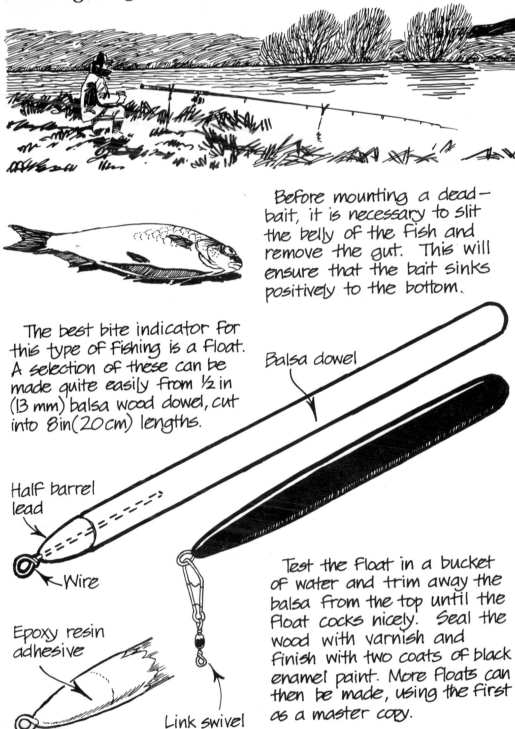

Before mounting a deadbait, it is necessary to slit the belly of the fish and remove the gut. This will ensure that the bait sinks positively to the bottom.

The best bite indicator for this type of fishing is a float. A selection of these can be made quite easily from ½ in (13 mm) balsa wood dowel, cut into 8in(20cm) lengths.

Balsa dowel

Half barrel lead

Wire

Epoxy resin adhesive

Test the float in a bucket of water and trim away the balsa from the top until the float cocks nicely. Seal the wood with varnish and finish with two coats of black enamel paint. More floats can then be made, using the first as a master copy.

Link swivel

Set-up for legered deadbait

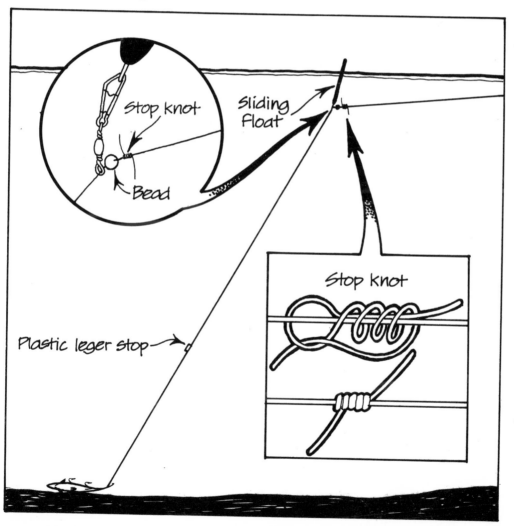

Stop knot

Bead

Sliding Float

Plastic leger stop

Stop knot

When a float is used in conjunction with a legered or paternostered bait, the stop knot should be set at a greater depth than the water. After the cast the rod tip is submerged and the line is lightly held by a line clip. The bale arm on the reel can be left in the open position.

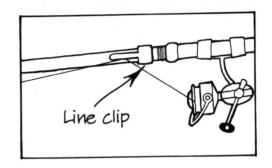

Line clip

Legered baits can also be freelined

Free lined leger bite indication set-up

Electronic bite indicator

'Monkey climb' indicator

Float paternoster set-up

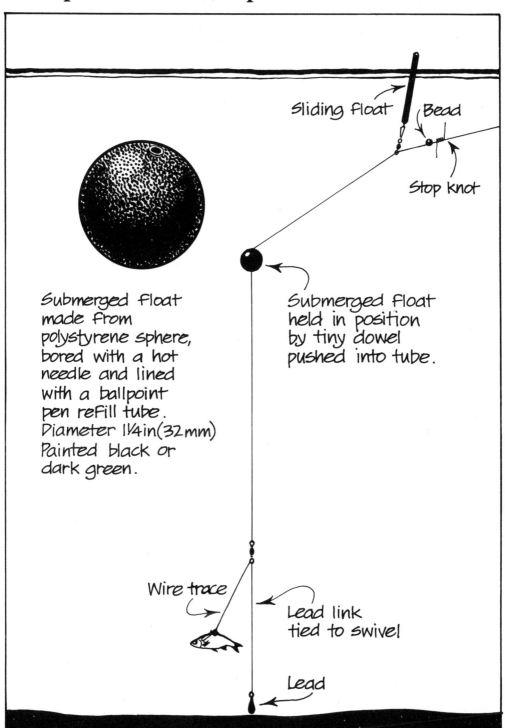

Sliding float

Bead

Stop knot

Submerged float made from polystyrene sphere, bored with a hot needle and lined with a ballpoint pen refill tube. Diameter 1¼in (32mm) Painted black or dark green.

Submerged float held in position by tiny dowel pushed into tube.

Wire trace

Lead link tied to swivel

Lead

Fishing a wobbled deadbait

During the autumn, shallow areas of a lake still support dense areas of bottom weed. These areas can be fished by working a deadbait just beneath the surface. Baits for this type of fishing should not be too large — 5in (12·5cm) is about right. To make the bait buoyant, insert a piece of polystyrene into the fish before it is mounted on the trace.

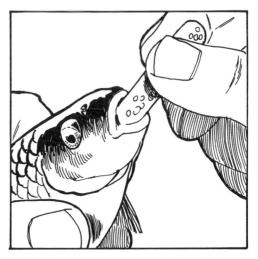

Wobble can be created by bending the body of the bait just before inserting the end treble. However, this can be overdone, producing an unnatural, gyrating motion when the bait is retrieved. The diagram(right) shows the subtle curve that is needed in order to produce the slow, natural, tumbling motion, typical of a wounded fish.

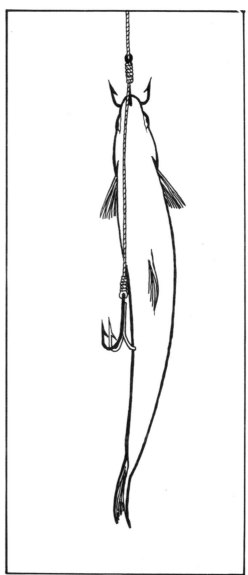

Sink-and-draw

Wobbled deadbaits can also be used with great effect to search areas of water, at any depth. This is best done by imparting a sink-and-draw motion to the bait. To produce the head down diving motion required of the bait fish, a modified terminal rig will have to be used.

Before the up-trace treble is tied to the wire trace, a length of fine wire should be soldered to the shank of the hook.

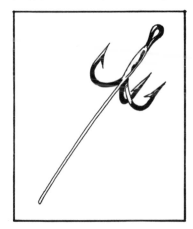

Lead pushed inside fish

The treble can then be tethered in the usual manner ......

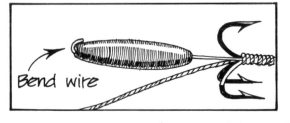

Bend wire

.... and a small barrel lead threaded on to the wire, and held in position as shown.

Lead-inserted deadbaits can be allowed to sink to the bed of the river or lake and retrieved very slowly.

As an alternative to having the weight inside the bait it can be positioned up-trace. This, however, may produce tangle problems if the correct type of rig is not used. The one shown here (used by Jim Gibbinson) is virtually tangle-free.

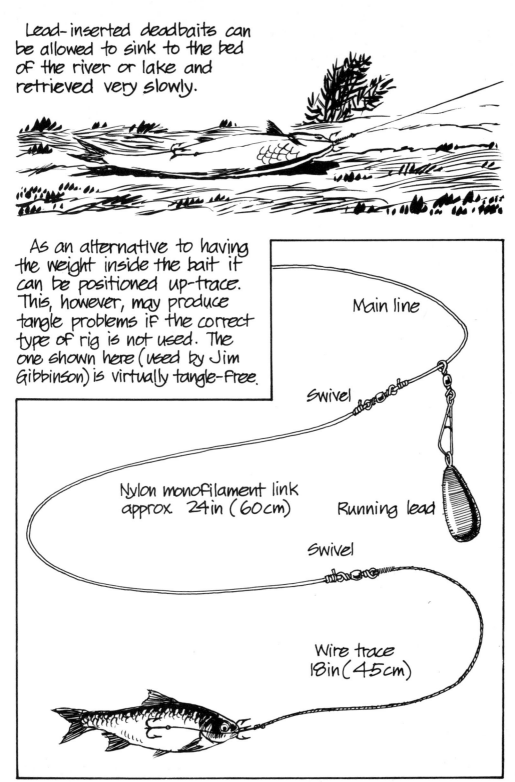

Main line

Swivel

Nylon monofilament link approx. 24in (60cm)

Running lead

Swivel

Wire trace 18in (45cm)

Drifting with a deadbait

This is a method which can be employed if the wind is blowing parallel to the shore, in an area with a good depth of water.

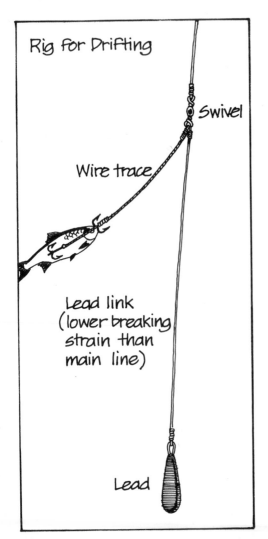

Rig for Drifting

Swivel

Wire trace

Lead link
(lower breaking strain than main line)

Lead

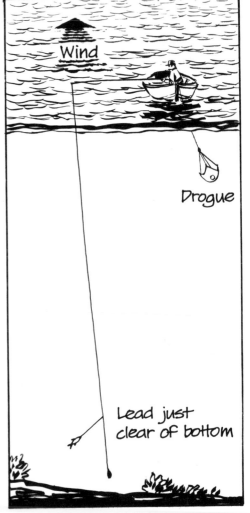

Wind

Drogue

Lead just clear of bottom

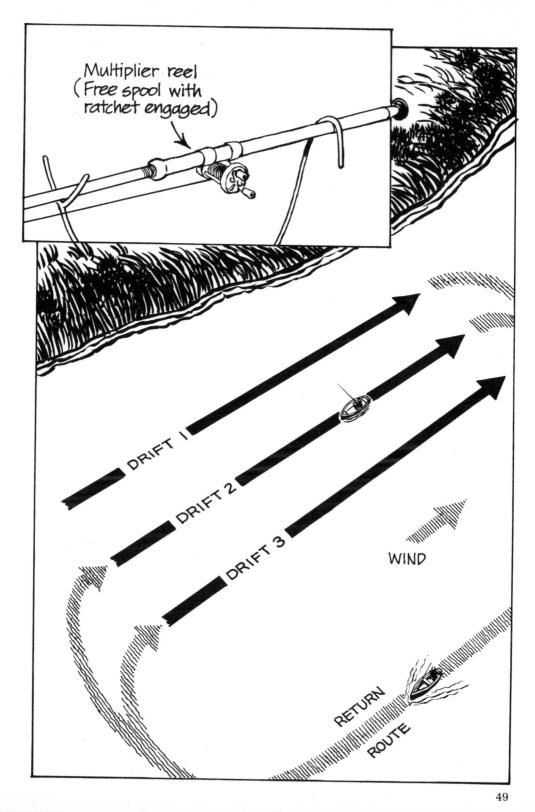

Fishing with a vaned float

Curved plastic vane (white)

Balsa body painted dark green

Eye

Brass rod stem

Eye whipped to stem

A vaned float is a useful addition to any pike angler's armoury, as it is capable, under the right weather conditions, of presenting the bait over a large area and at very long range.

The float is simple enough to make by using the materials shown. The one illustrated is a practical size, although it may be necessary to make an alternative, larger one for heavier use.

Float should self-cock to here.

Float should cock to here with bait and drilled bullet weight.

Extra weight can be provided by turns of lead wire on the stem.

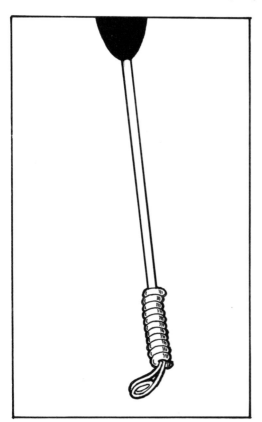

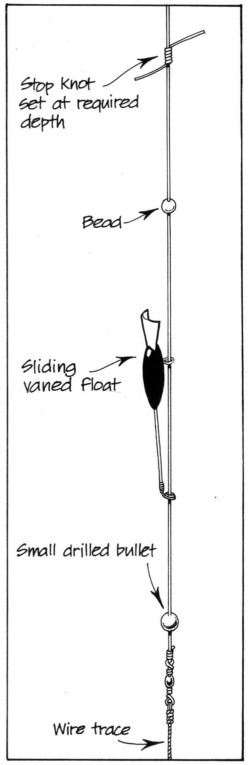

Stop knot set at required depth

Bead

Sliding vaned float

Small drilled bullet

Wire trace

The vaned float approach really comes into its own on waters which are bordered by impenetrable reeds. Some Norfolk Broads are a typical example of such waters. By anchoring a boat in a suitable position, a lot of water close to the reeds (a perfect pike-holding area) can be covered.

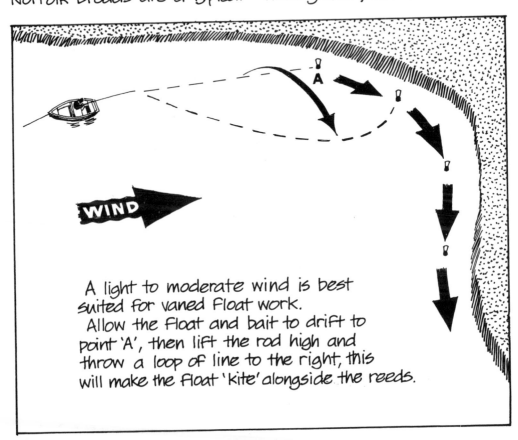

A light to moderate wind is best suited for vaned float work.
Allow the float and bait to drift to point 'A', then lift the rod high and throw a loop of line to the right, this will make the float 'kite' alongside the reeds.

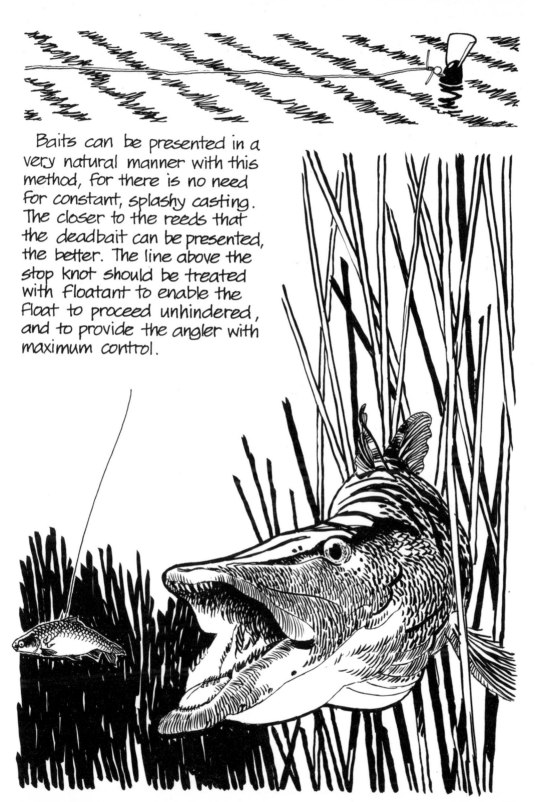

Baits can be presented in a very natural manner with this method, for there is no need for constant, splashy casting. The closer to the reeds that the deadbait can be presented, the better. The line above the stop knot should be treated with floatant to enable the float to proceed unhindered, and to provide the angler with maximum control.

Using a balloon for distance

On large reservoirs and lakes, pike-holding places may be beyond casting range. The solution to this problem is to harness a balloon to the terminal tackle and let the wind take it to the desired spot. The balloon can then be shaken off with a sharp, striking action of the rod, allowing the bait to sink to the bottom. The balloon will then come to rest against the downwind bank, from where it, and any other balloons, should be retrieved.

Paper clip

Treat the line with floatant, and with the reel in the free-line position allow the wind to take the balloon towards the target area.

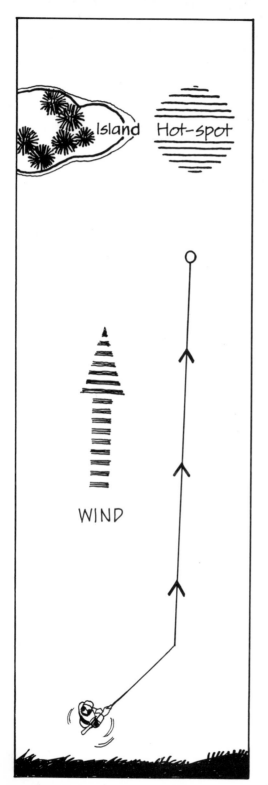

WIND

Island

Hot-spot

Strike off balloon here O

Island

Hot-spot

Boat fishing on large lakes

The large lochs of Scotland and Ireland, the Norfolk Broads, and reservoirs where pike exist are more effectively fished from a boat.

These areas of water are completely exposed to the elements, therefore it is vital that good-quality waterproof clothing is worn. The inclusion of a life-jacket is also a sensible precaution.

A weather report should always be obtained prior to venturing forth on to a very large lake.

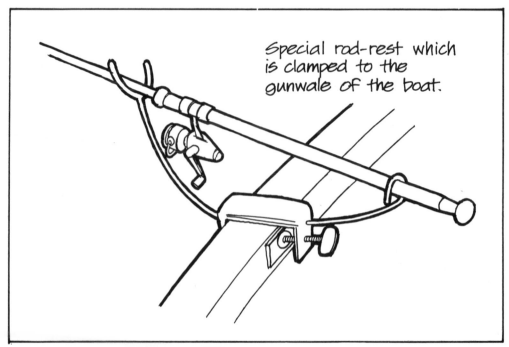

Special rod-rest which is clamped to the gunwale of the boat.

By using two of the special rod-rests shown opposite, two baits can be trolled at the same time. If the boat is anchored, as many as four rods can be fished at once.

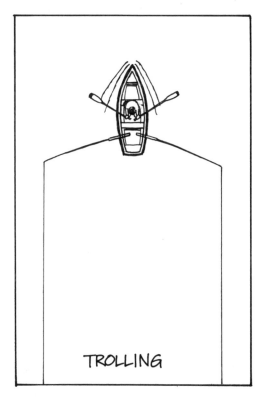

TROLLING

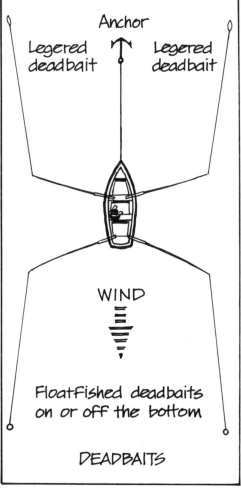

Anchor

Legered deadbait

Legered deadbait

WIND

Floatfished deadbaits on or off the bottom

DEADBAITS

Trolling

Some anglers consider this method to be boring; but it is, nevertheless, an ideal way of presenting a bait over large areas of water.

When trolling medium-depth waters the bait should be towed about 30 yd (27·5 m) behind a slowly-rowed boat.

Baits should always be gutted to ensure that they sink well.

RIGS

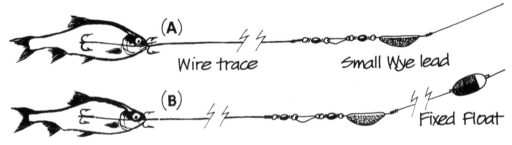

(A) Wire trace   Small Wye lead

(B)   Fixed Float

ROD SET-UP

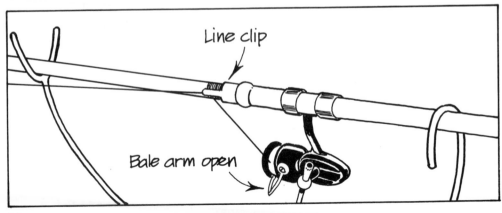

Line clip

Bale arm open

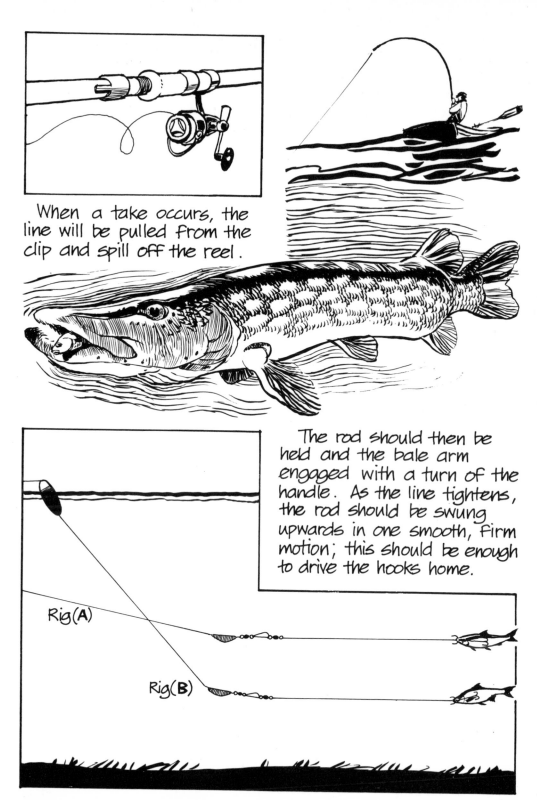

When a take occurs, the line will be pulled from the clip and spill off the reel.

The rod should then be held and the bale arm engaged with a turn of the handle. As the line tightens, the rod should be swung upwards in one smooth, firm motion; this should be enough to drive the hooks home.

Rig(**A**)

Rig(**B**)

Trolling in deep lakes is often done with a large centrepin reel, loaded with lead core line; but a multiplier, loaded with 15lb (7kg) nylon monofilament line, can also be used.

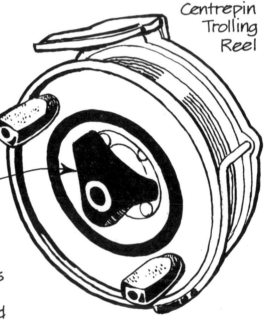

Centrepin Trolling Reel

The large drag knob can be set to any pressure required. The click of the ratchet will signal the presence of a taking pike.

If nylon monofilament line is being used, it will often be necessary to use a lead to hold the lure at the required depth.

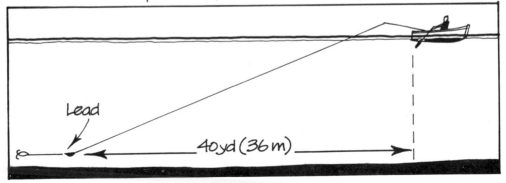

Lead

40yd (36 m)

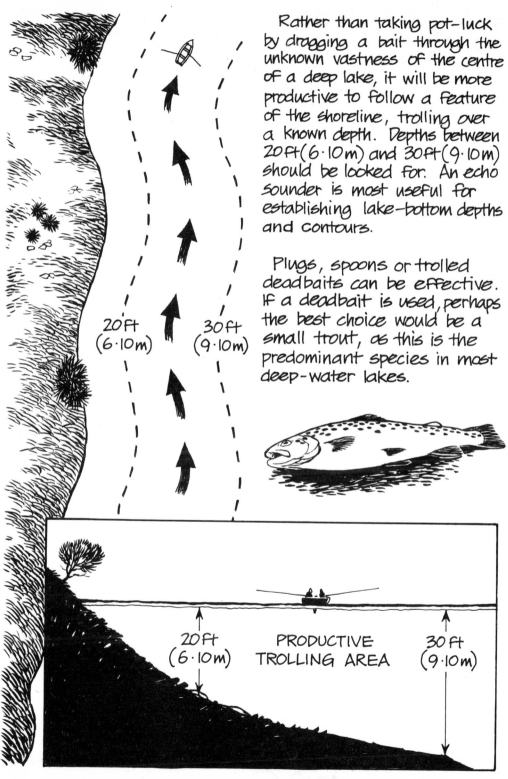

Rather than taking pot-luck by dragging a bait through the unknown vastness of the centre of a deep lake, it will be more productive to follow a feature of the shoreline, trolling over a known depth. Depths between 20ft (6·10m) and 30ft (9·10m) should be looked for. An echo sounder is most useful for establishing lake-bottom depths and contours.

Plugs, spoons or trolled deadbaits can be effective. If a deadbait is used, perhaps the best choice would be a small trout, as this is the predominant species in most deep-water lakes.

20ft
(6·10m)

30ft
(9·10m)

20ft
(6·10m)

PRODUCTIVE
TROLLING AREA

30ft
(9·10m)

Fly fishing for pike

Since the inception of the still-water trout fishing scene it has become very apparent that pike can be caught regularly on fly fishing tackle. It is therefore, a viable proposition for the angler to pursue the pike using the same tackle (with slight modification) that he would use for rainbow trout.

The 'flies' would have to be of the flashy, fry-imitating variety such as the examples I have shown.

Missionary

Appetizer

Baby Doll

Popper

The fly rod needs to be 9½ft–10ft (2·90m–3·05m) in length, with a line rating of 7–9.

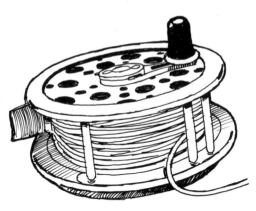

The reel needs to have a good line capacity such as that found on a salmon reel or a king-size lake trout reel. Plenty of backing line is needed, as it is not only the smaller pike that are attracted to feathered lures.

12lb–15lb (5·50kg–7kg) monofilament nylon

10in (25cm) nylon covered steel wire

The 'fly' can be attached to the leader via a small clip or spring link.

The fly tyer can produce many exotic variations for tempting pike.

Retrieve pike 'flies' fairly quickly, with an erratic motion.

Wearing a finger stall will prevent damage to the forefinger.

During the autumn, when weedgrowth still exists in the shallower bays, a popper fished with a floating line will prove very effective.

However, sub-surface 'flies' fished in conjunction with a sinking line will account for most pike.

Areas worth special attention
with a sunk 'fly' include :

CLOSE TO REEDS
OR RUSHES

WHERE FRY
ACTIVITY OCCURS

NEAR A SUNKEN
PIKEY FEATURE

Casting a fly

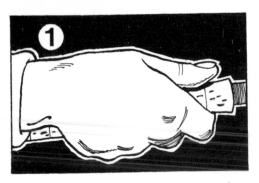

Hold the rod with the thumb on top of the handle....

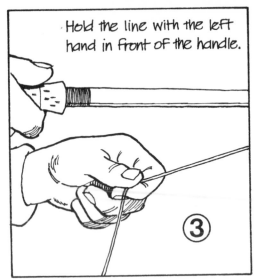

Hold the line with the left hand in front of the handle.

.... then pull enough line from the reel to provide enough weight to get the rod working properly.

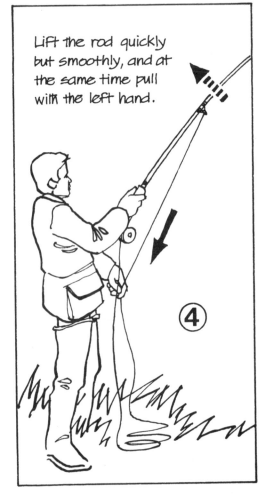

Lift the rod quickly but smoothly, and at the same time pull with the left hand.

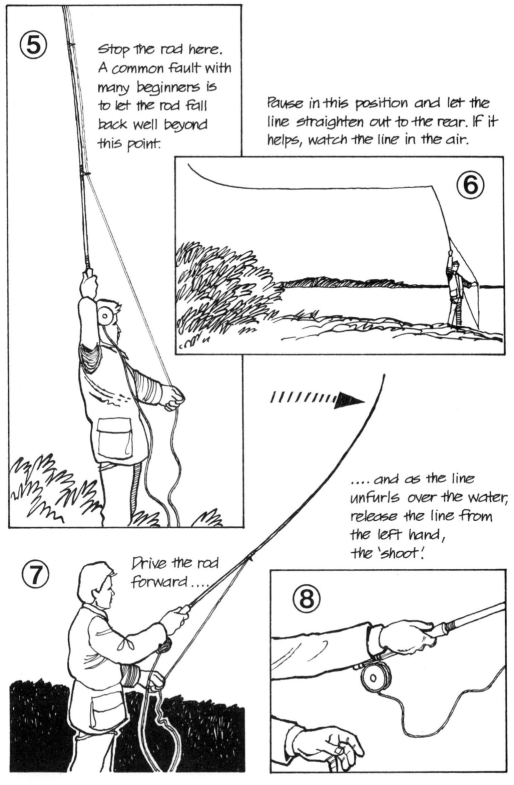

⑤ Stop the rod here. A common fault with many beginners is to let the rod fall back well beyond this point.

Pause in this position and let the line straighten out to the rear. If it helps, watch the line in the air.

⑥

⑦ Drive the rod forward.....

.... and as the line unfurls over the water, release the line from the left hand, the 'shoot'!

⑧

Home-made lures

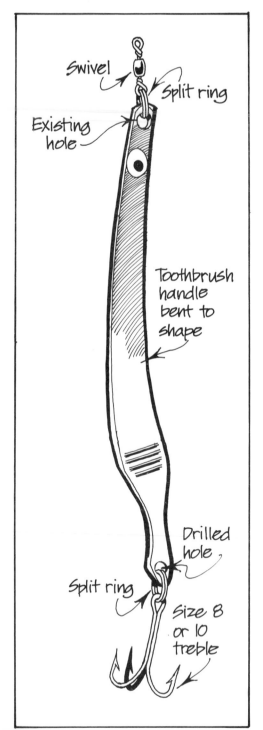

Swivel

Split ring

Existing hole

Toothbrush handle bent to shape

Drilled hole

Split ring

Size 8 or 10 treble

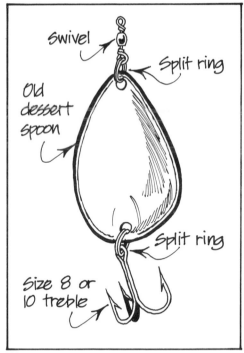

Swivel

Split ring

Old dessert spoon

Split ring

Size 8 or 10 treble

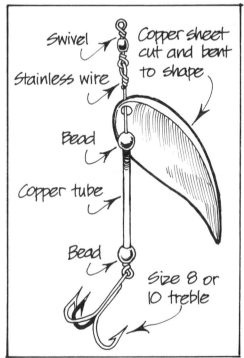

Swivel

Copper sheet cut and bent to shape

Stainless wire

Bead

Copper tube

Bead

Size 8 or 10 treble

Hooks

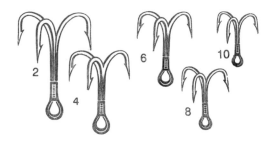

Good-quality treble hooks are vital where pike are concerned. When the angler tightens into a running fish he should be fully confident that the hook-point will, cleanly and efficiently, penetrate the bone and gristle of a pike's jaw. Recommended brands :– Mustad, Eagle Claw.

There is a considerate and common practice amongst good pike anglers to flatten two barbs on each treble hook. The fully-barbed hook is then used to secure the bait, while the other two hooks cope with the pike's jaws. Flattened barbs permit easy penetration and extraction, yet at the same time do not readily come adrift while the pike is being played.

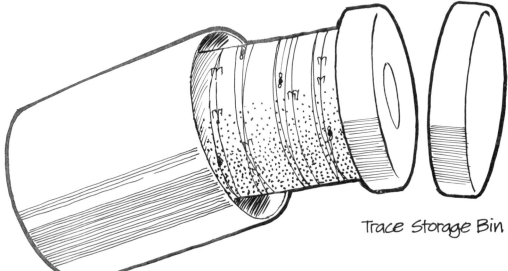

Trace Storage Bin

Hooking a pike

Hooking a pike on a lure poses no problems at all—suddenly, there he is on the end of the line. All that is then necessary is to maintain a firm, steady pressure to ensure that the hooks are driven firmly home.

Hooking a pike which has picked up a static deadbait is another kettle of fish. The prime consideration here is to attempt to hook the fish cleanly in the jaw, from where the hooks can be removed quickly and cleanly.

Hooking a pike on a deadbait

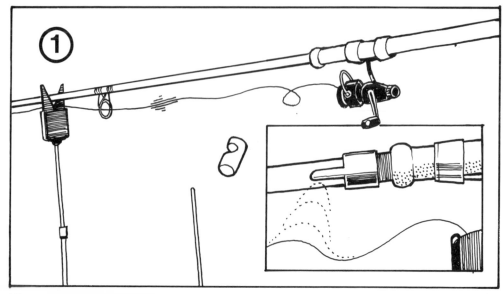

(1) The first sign of the presence of a pike may be no more than a twitch on the 'monkey' line or float, or a tentative 'bleep' on the electronic indicator, if one is being used. However, more often than not, the 'monkey' will fly off the needle, or the float slide beneath the surface and the line, pulled from the clip, will snake through the rod rings. This, of course, indicates that the pike has picked up the deadbait and is swimming away with it firmly clamped in his jaws.

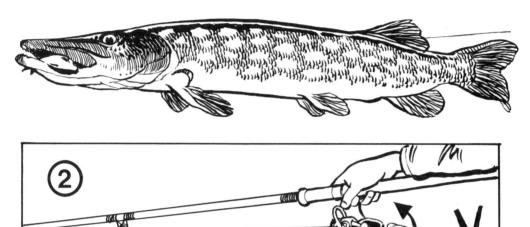

(2) The rod, still pointing on the same plane, should be lifted just clear of the rests. A turn on the reel handle will engage the bale arm.

(3) As the line pulls tight, lift the rod high. This should be enough to set the hooks. The process of playing the fish has now begun.

Playing a pike

The slipping-clutch on a fixed-spool reel and the star drag on a multiplier, should be set, prior to fishing, to yield line at a pressure below the breaking strain of the line being used. Finger or thumb pressure should also be applied to control the fish as it runs.

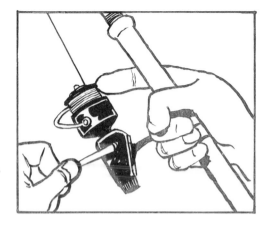

A running pike can usually be turned by sustained side-strain and firm finger or thumb pressure on the spool.

A pike which suddenly runs towards the angler can be a problem. Winding the reel handle rapidly and walking backwards at the same time will maintain contact with the fish until it turns again.

Hooked pike should always be kept well clear of snags and played out in a clear area of water.

Landing a pike

When a pike is beaten it will turn on its side. This is the time to draw it over the waiting net, which should be submerged and held stationary.

Lift the frame of the net clear of the water, grasp it with both hands and carry the net and fish clear of the water. Lay the fish on a soft, damp surface such as grass, moss, or a water-saturated sack.

Hook removal

Place a damp towel or a soft, damp sack over the fish. Gently trap the pike beneath this by kneeling astride it. This will prevent the pike thrashing about. Wear a leather gardening glove on the left hand.

Forceps

Put the index finger through the pike's gill slit and slide it towards the 'V' at the front of the lower jaw. Raise the pike's head from the ground whereupon it will open its mouth. Take the forceps in the right hand and slide them through the pike's gill slit. Take care not to damage the delicate gill rakers. Grip the shank of the hook with the forceps; turn the hook upside down and pull it free from the tissue.

Unhooking a lightly-hooked pike is more straightforward.

Weighing

Returning

Hold the fish in the water, on an even keel, until it swims away of its own accord.

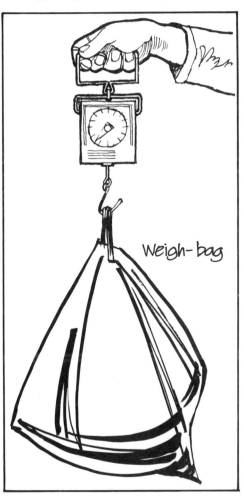

Weigh-bag

Loading a fixed spool reel

Pull knot tight before winding.

It is most important to load a fixed-spool reel with the correct amount of line. An incorrectly loaded reel will drastically reduce the distance of a cast.

Open the bale arm and secure the end of the line to the spool using a double slip knot.

Have someone holding the line spool and line as you wind the line on to the reel.

Face the spool towards the reel, and under gentle pressure, wind the line on to the reel spool. The reel is adequately loaded when the line level is about 1mm under the leading rim of the spool.

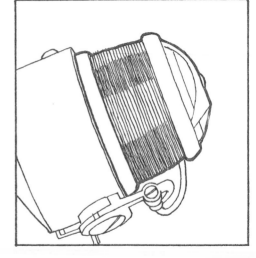

A correctly loaded reel.

Line

Good-quality line is a must where strong fish such as pike are the quarry. Strength of line required will vary from 9lb (4·00kg) to 12lb (5·50kg) breaking strain, or even 15lb (7kg) if the water is heavily-weeded.

Standard-size spools hold 110 yds (100m); bulk spools, 660 yds (600m).

Good line will fall limp from the spool. Harsh, springy line should never be used.

Very few knots are required in pike fishing as all hook connections are to wire, which is twisted or crimped. However a knot is still required to connect the main line to the swivel at the top of the wire trace. The one shown below is completely reliable.

TUCKED HALF-BLOOD KNOT

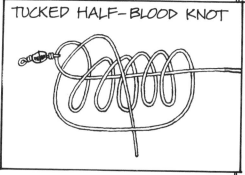

Home-made plug

Cut a length of hardwood dowel and drill a hole through the entire length.

Shape the body with a knife and fine sandpaper. Cut a groove to house the diving vane.

Drill a couple of holes in the underside of the body to accommodate two swan shot — these will act as ballast and keep the plug on an even keel. Ram the shot home and fill in the holes with plastic wood.

Fashion the diving vane from a piece of aluminium sheet and glue into the slot with epoxy adhesive. The body can now be painted.

Pass a length of 18 gauge stainless steel wire through the hole and form an eye at each end. Screw a small, brass screw eye into the underside of the body. Connect two size 10 treble hooks, with the aid of split rings, to the loop at the rear and to the screw eye beneath the body.

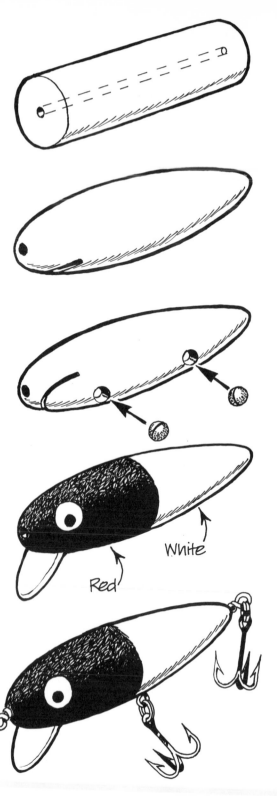

White

Red

Food for thought

This monstrosity (actual size) was created in Canada, for the purpose of fooling the great muskellunge, *Esox masquinongy*.

I purchased it from a fishing tackle shop in Picton, Ontario. The shop keeper told me that he had taken a 'musky' of 60 lb (27 kg) using one of these imitation musk rats.

The lure is made from deer hair and has two treble hooks. The eyes are represented by two green glass beads.

I can see no reason why it should not interest the larger pike in our European lakes — one day I may put it to the test.

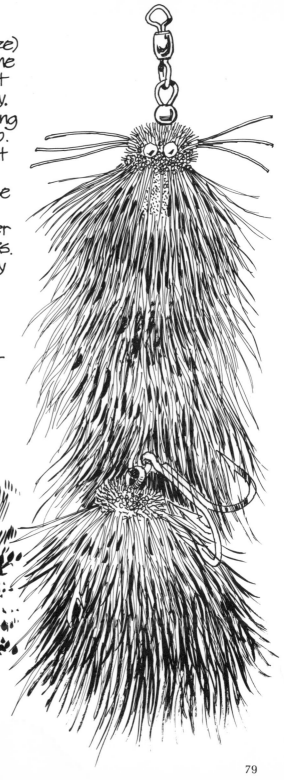